Original title:
Potted Poetry

Copyright © 2025 Creative Arts Management OÜ
All rights reserved.

Author: Fiona Harrington
ISBN HARDBACK: 978-1-80581-742-0
ISBN PAPERBACK: 978-1-80581-269-2
ISBN EBOOK: 978-1-80581-742-0

Flourish of Imagery

In pots so round, the plants do play,
They dance in sun, all through the day.
A cactus grins with spiky cheer,
While daisies gossip, oh so near.

A fern is twirling, quite a sight,
Its leafy limbs, a pure delight.
The violets chuckle, bloom with flair,
In this green world, no room for despair.

The Soil's Secret Songs

Deep in the dirt, where worms do roam,
The soil hums tunes, calling you home.
Each grain a note, a melody sweet,
Where radishes tap their little feet.

Potatoes sing of dreams down low,
While carrots giggle, taking it slow.
A shady root sings bass so low,
Nature's concert, a thrilling show.

Breathing in Blooms

In the morning light, blooms start to puff,
Petals expand, they can't get enough.
With each little sneeze, pollen takes flight,
Filling the air with tickly delight.

Sunflowers stretch, they reach for cheese,
While tulips giggle in the light breeze.
A daisy jokes, 'Don't be a thorn!'
In this garden, no one feels worn.

Chronicles in Clay

In pots of clay, tales are spun,
Where marigolds laugh and sunflowers run.
Their roots weave stories, bold and bright,
Of rainy days and dazzling light.

A weary sage shares wisdom true,
While lilacs plot another debut.
Each crack in the pot holds secrets old,
Of laughter, mischief, and a life bold.

A Palette of Prose

In a pot where words can sprout,
A cactus whispers, no need to shout.
With petals bright, they wriggle and tease,
Their stories twist in the summer breeze.

Laughing lilies in a row,
Giggle when the wind does blow.
Each line they bloom, a quirky sight,
Painting poems from day to night.

Hidden Harvests

Beneath the soil, where shadows play,
A turnip sings the blues today.
Radishes join, with hearts so bold,
Spilling secrets from roots of gold.

In every sprout, a tale in store,
Of veggies dreaming of folklore.
They dance and prance, under the sun,
Harvests hidden, but oh, such fun!

The Story Weaved in Stems

Once a vine with tales to tell,
Wrapped around a garden bell.
Its blossoms burst with giggles bright,
Whispering secrets in the night.

The thorns chuckle with pointed wit,
While beetles tap dance, never quit.
Each leaf unfurls a comic rhyme,
A story waiting, lost in time.

Resonance in Rains

Raindrops fall on a dancer's hat,
Splashing joy, imagine that!
Fungi jiggle, a spongy tune,
Under the light of a cheeky moon.

With every drop, a laugh erupts,
The soil hums as humor erupts.
Nature's symphony, a merry tune,
As laughter blossoms, afternoon to noon.

Rhyme in the Rain

Raindrops tap a silly song,
Umbrellas dance, all day long.
Splashing puddles, a footwear fight,
We laugh 'til we can't see right.

Wading through with squeaky shoes,
Finding joy in wet sock blues.
Clouds grumble like a grumpy cat,
Yet here we are, and that is that!

Stanzas in the Shade

Beneath the tree, we find our bliss,
A picnic nap turns into this.
Squirrels plot and birds scold loud,
While we munch snacks, feeling proud.

With lemonade in hand, we grieve,
For ants that steal, we can't believe!
Tanning toes while the sun plays tag,
Nature's antics — oh, what a rag!

Ephemeral Elegance

Daisies twirl in a breezy spree,
Butterflies join, what a sight to see.
Petals fall as the wind takes charge,
Nature's ballet, both small and large.

A dandelion makes a wish in flight,
Whoosh! Gone before the evening light.
We chase the whims of sweet decay,
In this garden, we laugh and play.

Nature's Narratives

The crickets chirp their evening tale,
As frogs croak out with great detail.
Fireflies flicker like tiny stars,
While raccoons plot, oh, how bizarre!

Leaves gossip as the branches sway,
Whispering secrets from yesterday.
We sit and soak in this vibrant show,
Nature's humor, in laughter, we grow!

Sonnet in Soil

In a pot with dirt, such dreams do sprout,
Worms do wiggle, just to check it out.
A cactus stole the show, quite bold and bright,
But heard a rumor, 'He's a prickly fright!'

Who knew a seed could tell such tales,
With petals dancing in the summer gales?
A lily laughed, 'Oh what a sight!',
As bees zoomed past, a dandelion in flight.

Budding Ballads

Little sprouts sing songs of sunny cheer,
With raindrops popping like a fizzy beer.
The soil's a stage for all to see,
While worms hum tunes, so whimsically.

'I'm a flower,' cried a weed with glee,
Petals painted bright, as bright can be.
But roots below just shake their heads,
'You're not invited to our fancy beds!'

Enchanted Terracotta

In pots of clay, the secrets lie,
With thousand tales that go awry.
A gnome with attitude stands tall and proud,
While spiders spin their webs around the crowd.

A vine tried tangoing with a fence,
But tripped on leaves, it made no sense!
The daisies chuckled, 'Such a show!',
As twirling stems put on a glow.

Lyrical Leaves

Leaves do whisper in the gentle breeze,
Tickling thoughts like secrets with ease.
A sunflower grinned—it grew so tall,
While daisies threw a plant-based ball.

Roots beneath gossip, 'What's the scoop?',
As Ladybug leads an outdoor troop.
When petals play and laughter's loud,
The garden's giggles attract a crowd!

Forked Paths of Poetry

At the garden's edge, words grow,
Some sprout up fast, some take it slow.
A tree of rhymes and puns invites,
Get lost in lines, like endless flights.

Branches twist, and jesters strut,
With quips and jabs, they laugh and cut.
Choose your route, will it be sweet?
Or do you prefer a prickly treat?

Beneath the shade, ideas play,
Frolicking in a sunny fray.
In plot twists where the laughter reigns,
Poetry wears its silliest chains.

So join the feast of curvy prose,
Where nonsense grows like wild rose.
A silly stroll through verses wide,
With laughter loud, our words abide.

Flourishing Fables

In a pot of tales, nonsense brews,
Garden gnomes wear flamboyant shoes.
With every line, absurdity dances,
Funny critters take their chances.

Fables bloom in colors bright,
Where cows can jump and stars take flight.
Chipmunks claim they write the rules,
While daisies hand out poetic tools.

With twisted plots and wild ideas,
A frog recites while juggling beers.
In every rhyme a jest concealed,\nMirrors of laughter are revealed.

So plant your words in soil of fun,
Under the bright and shining sun.
Nurtured with giggles, watered with cheer,
Flourishing fables, we hold dear.

Riddles in the Rhubarb

In rhubarb rows, a riddle grows,
With leafy whispers and playful shows.
What's green and sour, yet brings a cheer?
A fruit that hides; can you draw near?

Underneath the leaves, the fun begins,
With tricky truths and cheeky sins.
Why did the berry turn and flee?
Because it couldn't take a joke, you see!

Rhubarb's secret, or so they say,
Is to dance with words in a silly way.
It giggles, wiggles, without a care,
As riddles swirl in the fragrant air.

So pluck a line from this fruity patch,
And weave it into a playful match.
In the tangle of verse and vibrant humor,
Find joy in riddles, a sweet rumor.

Whimsy in the Weeds

In the weeds where mischief thrives,
Funny tales sprout like busy hives.
Dandelions laugh, and nettles tease,
With every line, we aim to please.

A ginger root that sings in tune,
While ladybugs dance beneath the moon.
Each weed a word that bends and sways,
In wacky ways through sunny days.

With every twist, a chuckle's near,
As blooms concoct a silly cheer.
Why did the weed refuse to grow?
It couldn't find a funny show!

So join the fun in overgrown plots,
Where whimsy reigns, and laughter knots.
In tangled verses, carefree and bold,
A garden of giggles, ever untold.

Whispering Willows

In the garden, secrets play,
Where willows giggle every day.
They sway and bend with glee so loud,
Joking with the passing cloud.

Beneath their shade, the squirrels dance,
Chasing leaves in their wild prance.
The breeze carries a playful tune,
As flowers laugh beneath the moon.

In the sunlight, petals wink,
While bees sing sweet with every blink.
The trees conspire, oh what a sight,
In the garden of pure delight.

So if you wander, heed their call,
Join the fun, and laugh with all.
For nature's humor, rich and free,
Is the best kind of poetry!

Fragrant Feelings

Petals blush in colors bright,
Each daisy grins with sheer delight.
A fragrance wafts, it tickles noses,
As garden gnomes hold funny poses.

Rosemary winks with fragrant charm,
While mint teases with a cooling balm.
The lilacs giggle, oh so strong,
Making noses dance along.

In this patch, joy seems to bloom,
As honeybees plot to steal the room.
With nectar sweet, their laughter flows,
In this world where no one knows.

So stop and smell, embrace the cheer,
Let nature's humor draw you near.
For in each whiff, a laugh you'll find,
A fragrant riddle, sweet and kind.

The Verse of Vines

Twisting, turning, up they climb,
These laughing vines keep perfect time.
With every loop, a jest they spin,
In the sun's glow, their giggles begin.

They tangle with each other tight,
Creating a scene of pure delight.
From leaf to leaf, whispers weave,
In this tangled tale, none can grieve.

The grapes chuckle, juicy and sweet,
As crickets join in on their beat.
With every flicker, a dance of cheer,
Vines frolic as the dusk draws near.

So wander through this leafy dream,
Where humor flows like a silver stream.
In every twist and playful sway,
The vines will surely steal your way.

Echoes of Earth

From the soil, a chuckle rises,
As worms tell jokes in their disguises.
With every root, a tale unfolds,
Of garden banter, brave and bold.

The daisies boast of sunny glee,
While rocks crack jokes, as stony as can be.
The grass below makes silly sounds,
As laughter echoes round and round.

In this land, delight is true,
The daisies dance, the skies are blue.
While crickets chirp a merry tune,
Beneath the watchful, smiling moon.

So step outside, hear nature's cheer,
In every whisper, life's dear.
For in this garden, joy takes root,
Echoes of laughter, oh, so cute!

Beats of Botanics

In the garden, plants do dance,
Wobbling leaves, they take a chance.
Rooted jesters in sunlit hats,
Listen closely to their chats.

Cacti crack jokes, quite a prick,
While daisies giggle, quick and slick.
Tomatoes blushing, oh so red,
With puns that sprout right from their bed.

Worms in suits attend the show,
Wiggling to the rhythm's flow.
Sunshine beams, bright and bold,
Tales of green, endlessly told.

At dusk, the garden's tunes do fade,
But laughter lingers, never swayed.
A symphony of roots and leaves,
In this wacky world, no one grieves.

Prose Among Petals

Petals whisper, secrets shared,
While bees plot mischief, quite prepared.
Lilies laugh and swirl around,
In a swirl of colors, joy is found.

Butterflies wearing polka dots,
Flutter about and tie their knots.
Gardener chuckles, seeds in hand,
As blooms erupt at his command.

The tulips tell of fashion trends,
In hues and prints that break all bends.
Roses blushing, full of glee,
Dream of dating a bumblebee.

At sunset, all their tales unfold,
In laughter and joy, strong and bold.
Every petal has a tale to weave,
In this garden where we believe.

Twined Tales in Green

Vines entwine in a tangled mess,
Whispering gags, oh, what a press!
Climbing high with giggly glee,
The soil shakes with their decree.

Sprouts in rows, a comedy club,
Each one waiting for its scrub.
Carrots joke, stretch, and smile,
While radishes dance in a funky style.

Not a weed in sight to fear,
Just laughter that you'll overhear.
Garden gnomes, they cheer and clap,
As the squash join in with a laugh.

Underneath a sunlit beam,
Joyous laughter becomes the theme.
Among the green, they dream and play,
In this leafy cabaret.

A Symphony of Seedlings

In the dirt, a party brews,
Buds and leaves in joyful hues.
Sprouts are jiving, cannot stop,
With daffodils spinning on top.

Buttercup beats, a wild refrain,
Dancing petals, free from pain.
A sunflower struts, tall and proud,
Its lofty jokes lift the crowd.

In a pot, a soil symphony,
Giggling roots sway in harmony.
Each seedling's song in playful tone,
In this green realm, nobody's alone.

Even when night begins to creep,
The laughter stays, the roots don't sleep.
A crescendo of life, bold and bright,
In the garden, everything feels right.

Stems of Thought

In a pot, my thoughts do dance,
Wiggling 'round, they take a chance.
With every twist, they set a show,
Who knew my brain could grow and glow?

Sunshine flickers, rain drops sound,
A garden party underground.
The worms, they gossip, seeds conspire,
Each tiny sprout's a budding fire.

A quirky weed joins in the fray,
Says, "I'm artistry!"
Mischievous petals break the rules,
Who needs a zephyr? Just let it drool.

Oh, roots entangled in a plot,
Making mischief, they tie the knot.
With humor's help, they sprout and jest,
Life's a potluck; bring your best!

Words Beneath the Surface

In the soil, whispers sprout,
Turnip tales and bean-dream clout.
Radishes giggle, carrots laugh,
Each leafy line's a hearty gaffe.

Sunlight's tickle brings a grin,
Funny puns, where to begin?
Chives are cheeky, basil's bright,
Sassy herbs in fragrant flight.

Underneath where roots entwine,
Puns grow wild, a grand design.
Plant a joke, and watch it bloom,
Crack a smile in this green room.

So here's a riddle for the wise,
What's orange, round, and causes sighs?
A pumpkin's punchline, sure to please,
Just sow some laughter with the peas!

The Garden's Gossamer

In the garden, threads are spun,
Tangled tales of frolicking fun.
Butterflies weave jokes in the air,
While daisies giggle without a care.

Petal parties, oh what a sight!
Ferns do the limbo, all night bright.
Each bloom's a punchline, each bud a jest,
Laughing together, the flowers fest.

Squirrels gossip, a whimsical scene,
Chasing their tails on the green machine.
Caterpillars punk in their stylish homes,
Dressed up in stripes, they gather gnomes.

With every gust, the stories flow,
Nature's humor puts on a show.
In this riot of blooms, take a chance,
Join the laughter, join the dance!

Inked in Earth

With ink of mud, I write my verse,
Each rhyme comes out a bit diverse.
My fingers stained, a splotchy delight,
Nature's quill boosts the mood tonight.

Flora scribbles, petals in a row,
Blooms are stylists, ready to show.
Sprouts and shoots in clever lines,
Chortles of laughter in tangled twines.

The beetles read my leafy prose,
Scribbling dreams from their tiny toes.
A butterfly flits, adds flair with grace,
Penning its thoughts on a dewy lace.

In garden plots, my words take root,
Shaped by giggles, they bear sweet fruit.
So let's dig deep, let humor churn,
In the earth, there's much to learn!

Soil and Sonnet

In a garden of giggles, the soil does chuckle,
With worms doing waltzes, and frogs in a huddle.
A sunflower in shades, like a clown with a grin,
It sways in the breeze, letting silliness in.

Gloves on my hands, I dig with delight,
The dirt gives me riddles, so silly and bright.
Each shovel a stanza, a verse from the ground,
Where laughter is sown, and joy is profound.

A radish rethinks its role in this play,
'Why not wear roses on my roots,' it will say.
The carrots stand tall in their orange parade,
As peas giggle softly, in their green masquerade.

So here's to the soil, our poetic friend,
Where laughter and growth intertwine and blend.
With each turn of earth, a rhyme we will find,
In this funny old garden, where whimsy's unconfined.

Roots of Rhyme

Down in the dirt, where the roots start to dance,
Worms wiggle and writhe, in a wiggly trance.
A dandelion dreams of a soft, cushy bed,
While sunbeams tickle its perky green head.

The beetles write ballads on the bark of a tree,
While the grass does the cha-cha, as happy as can be.
Chattering leaves share secrets of lore,
In the land of the roots, there's always much more.

A potato thinks 'bout fanciful hats,
While turning raps with the giggling rats.
Each seed has a story, a laugh or a joke,
In this goofy old garden, where dreams come to poke.

So let's uproot boredom, with a burst of delight,
In a world spun with humor, from morning to night.
With roots intertwined, the rhymes grow wide,
In the soil of our dreams, where giggles abide.

Petals and Pages

Petals flutter like pages in a breezy old book,
Each flower is story, if you stop just to look.
The daisies gossip, in whispers so sweet,
While the roses spill secrets, from down by their feet.

In the garden of laughter, where colors collide,
The tulips wear hats with such flair and such pride.
A daffodil dances, with a twirl and a spin,
As the lilac laughs bright, with a chuckle within.

The sun's like a jester, with rays on its crown,
It tickles the blooms, making all frown upside down.
With petals as pages, let's write something new,
In the tale of the garden, there's always a clue.

So let's read the riddle that blossoms each day,
In the funny old garden, where merriment plays.
For every bright petal, and page that we turn,
There's laughter and joy, for us all to learn.

Verses in Vases

A vase holds a story, of colors and cheer,
With flowers that chatter, for all who come near.
The daisies are jesters, giggling away,
While the lilies declare, 'Let's party today!'

Each stem has a tale, from the roots to the top,
The tulips are telling their funny old bop.
In this glass full of humor, let's dance in a line,
With petals like verses, in rhythms divine.

The hydrangeas grumble about rain and the sun,
While the sunflowers giggle, 'We're all here for fun!'
With water like ink, filling all up to the brim,
The flowers unite, in a whimsical whim.

So here's to the verses that flourish and bloom,
In the vases of laughter, where silliness looms.
From roots to the petals, the joy does embrace,
In the garden of giggles, in this merry-place.

Treasures in Terracotta

In a pot so round, a dream takes root,
With a cheeky sprout, in a tiny suit.
Cacti in hats, succulents in shoes,
They gossip about the world's mundane views.

A dandelion strutted, its fluff on display,
Claiming it's royalty, come what may.
With twirls and with sways, it danced the night,
While daisies laughed, in pure delight.

Moss got jealous, grew a beard so long,
Complaining the flowers all sing the wrong song.
They giggled and cheered, "Oh, let's have a jam!
We'll play on the porch, bring a carrot or ham!"

So in this old pot, tales bloom and sway,
Each plant has a story, each leaf has a say.
With laughter and roots, they sway in the breeze,
In a garden of wonders, they do as they please.

Hearth of Harmony

In a corner so cozy, lush greens arise,
Chasing the sun with ambitious sighs.
A chubby fern claims the softest chair,
While the violets giggle, without a care.

The thyme tells jokes, it's a real wit,
While parsley and sage give each other a hit.
With witty remarks, they turn up the fun,
In this silly space, under the warm sun.

A pot of marigolds mismatched in hues,
Decide they'll throw in their own quirky views.
One shouts about drama, another about cheer,
"Let's toast to the day with a brew, my dear!"

Amidst the warmth, a cactus rolls its eyes,
"Who invited these flowers? It's no surprise!"
But laughter erupts, as the sun starts to set,
In the hearth of this garden, with no hint of regret.

The Beauty in Blooms

A daisy stood tall, with a wink and a grin,
"Check out my petals, just let the fun begin!"
A passing bee buzzed, "You fancy or what?"
"Just living my best, in this cheerful spot!"

Petunias chimed in, all frilled and neat,
"Without a good laugh, we'd be incomplete!"
They painted the pot in colors so bright,
Creating a masterpiece, pure delight!

"Who's got the jokes?" asked a shy little sprout,
"I'll tell one now, let me figure it out!"
But before it could speak, the lilies nearby,
Burst into laughter, oh my, oh my!

In the warmth of the pot, a friendship did bloom,
Filled with tales and giggles, it banished all gloom.
So here in this pot, laughter always glows,
In a vibrant community, where hilarity flows.

Melodies of the Meadow

A pot in the corner begins to hum low,
With melodies sweet, as the breezes blow.
The herbs join the chorus, all waving their leaves,
"Let's sing our hearts out, like nobody believes!"

"Thyme's got a tune, and basil's a star,
With rhythms so catchy, they'll travel afar.
Cilantro and mint, doing a tap dance,
While the chamomile twirls, in a happy romance."

The daisies burst forth with a cheeky refrain,
"Life's too short, let's dance in the rain!"
A sunflower cheered, "Let's break into song,
Together in laughter, that's where we belong!"

As night starts to fall, they gather round tight,
Sharing the tales of the day's funny plight.
In a meadow of giggles, echoes and glee,
This pot of joy sings of life's harmony.

Inkwell of Iris

In a garden of quips, the ink takes flight,
Petals in laughter, oh what a sight.
A worm takes a sip, says, "Is this a joke?"
While daisies giggle, their stems all bespoke.

With words like confetti, they dance and twine,
Each line a sprout, as silly as wine.
A cactus chortles, with needles so keen,
Wishing he could wear a hat made of green.

The roses roll over, bursting with cheer,
Swapping their secrets, the neighbors can hear.
A daffodil winks, says, "Life's just a play!"
While bees buzz along, laughing all day.

So let's tip our teacups, let laughter escape,
For every petal's a tale in good shape.
In this ink-filled realm where the silliness flows,
The fun never dims, as the garden still grows.

Stitched by Sunbeams

Sunshine stitches dreams onto petals so bright,
Laughter weaves colors in every warm light.
A dandelion chuckles, as wishes take flight,
While shy violets blush at the sight of delight.

Jokes bloom like daisies, sprouting all around,
With giggles and jokes in the air abound.
A sunflower nods, as if in on the fun,
Says, "Life's a fine quilt, stitched under the sun!"

The tulips prance, in a silly ballet,
Twisting and turning, oh what a display!
While garden gnomes grin, sparkling with glee,
In this patch of laughter, come join the spree!

So here's to the stitches that bind us in mirth,
In this sunny realm, oh what joy and worth!
With sunbeams to guide, together we play,
Creating a quilt that brightens our day.

Brews of Blooming Rhyme

In the kettle of blooms, a rhyme starts to brew,
Laughter pours forth, like morning dew.
A rose whispers softly, with petals all bright,
"What's brewing today? Oh, it feels just right!"

The daisies are stirring, with giggles so light,
Adding a pinch of pure delight.
A snapdragon chuckles, breathes fire in the mix,
Says, "Hold onto your hats, let's give them a fix!"

With honeybee dancers, flitting around,
They swirl in the breeze, with joy unbound.
A sprinkle of whimsy, a dash of good cheer,
In this pot of blooms, let the laughter draw near!

So sip on the joy, let the giggles collide,
In this brew of blooming, no reason to hide.
For every small petal is bursting with rhyme,
In a garden so silly, we dance through the thyme.

The Color of Composition

With strokes of the brush, the colors collide,
A symphony bright, where the giggles reside.
Brushes like worms, wriggle and sway,
Painting the laughter in their own silly way.

A canvas of daisies, dipped in pure fun,
Each bloom a line, under the sun.
The paint splatters joy, like confetti on air,
While tulips paint whispers without a care.

Palette of chuckles, mixed green and gold,
Stories in colors, waiting to unfold.
With laughter as colors, we dance and we play,
Crafting a masterpiece of bright, silly sway.

So gather the hues, let the rainbow grow wide,
In this colorful chaos, there's nowhere to hide.
For the art of our laughter will never grow old,
In the gallery of joy, let our stories be told!

Verses Underfoot

In the garden, where weeds dance,
A poem sprouts, given a chance.
With muddy dreams, they take a leap,
And laughter blooms, the soil's keep.

The gnomes giggle and wink with glee,
As lines go wild and twist like a tree.
The daisies join in, what a sight!
Singing verses from morning till night.

Each petal whispers a secret tune,
Beneath the bright and chuckling moon.
The worms nod along, they're quite the fans,
As rhyme takes root in quirky plans.

So after rain, when sunbeams crawl,
Those verses underfoot stand tall.
They tickle toes and spin a tale,
Of life in the soil, where dreams sail.

The Fauna's Embrace

In the shade where critters conspire,
A squirrel recites with sprightly fire.
His acorn hat tilts, what a show,
As rabbits hop, not feeling too slow.

The hedgehog jots down a clever quip,
While beetles join in with a tiny sip.
Each line, a tickle, each word, a flight,
In the laughter of beasts, the world feels right.

The fox in glasses grins by the brook,
Crafting lines from a well-worn book.
While frogs ribbit, with joy they croak,
In this wild jest, the woods invoke.

As dawn breaks bright, their laughter remains,
In nature's book, not one thought contains.
The fauna's embrace, a playful spree,
Where poetry blooms, wild and free.

Roots of Rhyme

Down below where the roots digest,
A tangle of thoughts finds its rest.
Each worm writes lines with a wiggly twist,
In a hidden world where none can resist.

The soil chuckles with every beat,
As it sways to the rhythm of tiny feet.
The beetles declare, "This is our time!"
In the dance of the dark, they find their rhyme.

The turnips hum with a full-bellied laugh,
Rooted tightly in their charming staff.
As carrots dream of a rhyming spree,
In the depths of the earth, they're wild and free.

Under the ground, where the secrets creep,
Lies an orchestra's joy, in laughter they leap.
With whispers of fun, in shadows they climb,
The roots of the earth give birth to rhyme.

Metaphors in Moss

On a log where the moss grows bold,
Lie metaphors wrapped in tales untold.
Each squishy green patch forms a line,
A wet giggle from nature, divine.

Amongst the ferns, the laughter spreads,
As toadstools nod in their snoozy beds.
With every squelch and every squish,
Mossy tales come true, just like a wish.

The snails slip past, with thoughts profound,
Carrying verse on their slow, soft ground.
While fireflies blink in a twinkling jest,
At these metaphors, they simply rest.

So here in the shade, with joy in the air,
The forest speaks with a playful flair.
Where moss holds verses, old and new,
In the laughter of nature, there's always a clue.

Petals and Pages

In a garden where the laughter grows,
Petals dance with the wind that blows.
Pages rustle, words take flight,
In this soil of joy, everything's bright.

A daisy told a joke to a rose,
The tulips giggled, striking a pose.
A violet blushed, so shy and sweet,
As bees buzzed in with a rhythmic beat.

Laughter ripples through leafy vines,
Whimsical tales tucked in the spines.
With roots that tickle and stems that sway,
Each bloom has something funny to say.

So grab a pot, let the humor grow,
In this laughter-filled botanical show.
With petals blushing from giggles wild,
Join the fun, be nature's child.

Syllables in Succulents

Succulent smiles in ceramic halls,
Chortling cacti in their tiny stalls.
Words sprout like shoots, so green and round,
In this playful patch, joy is found.

Each syllable sways with a gentle jig,
As pot plants prance, all part of the gig.
Laughter bubbles in pots of clay,
With each new joke, plants shout 'Hooray!'

A rogue fern sneaked in with a pun,
Silencing the daisies, they cried, 'How fun!'
The thyme tickles with fragrant quips,
While rosemary dances, doing flips.

In this garden, words grow tall,
Beneath the sun, we hear them call.
So join the crew of this green ensemble,
Where language blooms and laughter rambles.

A Wreath of Words

A circle of leaves, a crown of cheer,
Whispers of joy fill the atmosphere.
Wreathed in verses, crafted with glee,
Nature's punchlines set us free.

Twisting vines, a cleverly spun tale,
Each line drips with humor, never stale.
The bark tells stories, the blooms relate,
Of awkward plants and their goofs innate.

With petals chuckling, the daisies spread,
The roses giggle, their colors red.
A sassy sunflower supporters applause,
For every fresh quip without a pause.

As we gather round this leafy display,
Savor the laughter that brightens the day.
A wreath of words, so fluffy and light,
In this garden of fun, everything's right.

The Seedling Symphony

In a patch of sun, seedlings take the stage,
Performing giggles, setting the gauge.
With tiny roots, they stomp and cheer,
Creating a symphony for all to hear.

A dandelion croons a silly tune,
With melodies sweet as a bright afternoon.
The petunias sway with elegant grace,
As laughter erupts in this happy space.

Tiny sprouts whisper in giddy delight,
Their playful banter an echoing flight.
With every note sung, more joy is sown,
In this seedling cast, you're never alone.

So come join this joyful green ballet,
With every petal dancing, come out and play.
In the symphony of life, let's all partake,
With seedlings laughing, we'll never forsake.

The Nurtured Narrative

In a pot, a plant held court,
Telling tales of leaves so short.
Sunshine rays and water glee,
Oh, the stories it would see!

A worm once asked for a raise,
But star plants are the ones that craze.
'Grow up tall!' they'd all proclaim,
While the peas just played a game.

Dandelions joined the brawl,
Their fluffy heads just loved to sprawl.
In their garden, laughter bloomed,
As mischief danced, bright and groomed.

Chasing roots beneath the soil,
While ladybugs would simply toil,
With little pots on every shelf,
They grew their dreams, none like themselves!

Echoes from the Herb Bed

Basil whispers to the thyme,
'What's your secret? Share the rhyme!'
Sage jumped in with a cheeky grin,
'Round here, it's all about the spin!'

Oregano tossed in some flair,
As chives danced with a fragrant air.
Even garlic laughed so loud,
Transforming soil into a crowd.

The mint was sly, oh what a tease,
'Taste my leaves, you'll feel the breeze!'
Rosemary blushed, as friends would cheer,
In this herb bed, fun was near!

With every pot, a story spun,
Echoes of joy meant laughter won.
Greens unite in a quirky tale,
For herbivores that never pale!

Fragrant Fables

Once in a pot, a flower would say,
'Tell tales of joy all night and day!'
Marigolds cheered, with petals spread,
While daisies nodded, their faces red.

A cactus chimed, 'I'm sharp but nice!'
The others laughed, 'Oh, that's a slice!'
Succulents joined with a gentle sway,
Spreading laughs in their own silly way.

'What's in a dream?' the violets sang,
'With roots so deep, our hearts just hang!'
And in the evening light so bright,
Their fragrant fables took to flight.

With every word, the garden brightened,
As fantasies of bloom ignited.
In this patch where humor grows,
Fragrant fables, a garden prose!

The Ode of Outdoors

In the outdoors, pots sit proud,
Their leafy heads above the crowd.
Sunshine tickles, rain will play,
Laughter bursts, come what may!

A rogue weed thought it'd invade,
But pots just giggled, unafraid.
'You can try, but we're a team!'
And so they sang, a verdant dream.

A butterfly flitted, quite the show,
'How do you grow? Let me know!'
Herb pots shrieked with tales galore,
As nature laughed, they yearned for more.

With every breeze, they shared delight,
Crickets chirped into the night.
In the garden, joy's out loud,
The ode of outdoors, forever proud!

Serene Stanzas

In a little pot, I tried some dirt,
Planted my dreams, all crisp and alert.
Watered them well, forgot the sun,
Now they all groan, 'This isn't fun.'

A cactus appeared, sharp as a thumb,
I asked it for wisdom, it just went 'Dumb!'
In this little space, I grow my laughs,
Hoping my daisies will make me dance half.

Tiny herbs whisper their leafy jokes,
Chives and thyme, those clever folks.
I chuckle along, it's quite the scene,
Who knew plants could be such a meme?

Once I grew beans, oh, what a twist,
Out of their shells, they made quite a list.
I watch them sprout, their comedy roots,
In this green little world, I gather my hoots.

Remnants of Rooted Revelations

Here's to the flowers, a riot of cheer,
One sneezed at me, said, 'Stay clear, dear!'
A tulip twirled, in a dance quite bizarre,
She said, 'Life's short, be your own superstar!'

Basil is bossy, always in charge,
Critiques my salad, says it's too large.
Mint chortles softly, its laughter is cool,
While sage sits back, acting all wise in school.

One day I'll grow, a tree full of glee,
But right now, it's just my pots and me.
We're cultivating humor in this small space,
With roots in the ground, and joy on our face.

So if you should find your plant's got a quirk,
Don't fret too much, embrace the work.
For in every leaf and each tiny sprout,
There's laughter to find—just look about!

Threads of Thorny Ink

In the garden of wit, I plant a thought,
With ideas that twist like a silly knot.
The thorns of my humor prick at the core,
As laughter blooms wildly, who could want more?

Write a poem on a leaf, let it sprout,
Watch it dance in the wind, laughing out loud.
With roots deep in giggles, they wiggle and weave,
Each line like a vine that just won't leave.

The ink spills like water, a puddle of cheer,
It drips and it hitchhikes, brings smiles near.
So grab your pen, let the jest begin,
In this patch of absurd, we're all sure to win.

A tangle of phrases, a glorious mess,
In the soil of the silly, we find our excess.
So here in my plot, with a chuckle and wink,
We spread the good fun with threads of thorny ink.

Poetry Bursting from Pots

In the corner of the room, pots stacked high,
Each one a secret, watch words fly.
With a wiggle and jiggle, they jump out with glee,
Like colorful fireworks, wild and free.

A poem in a flowerpot, blooming in rhyme,
Sprouting up quickly, no need for time.
They giggle in whispers, share with a grin,
While the gardener of laughter tosses them in.

With a sprinkle of humor, the dirt is all smiles,
Each seed is a punchline, sowing in styles.
A bloom here, a chuckle there, what a great mix,
These quirky creations are all of our tricks.

So come, gather round, and don't you forget,
In the land of the funny, there's no room for regret.
With pots overflowing, we laugh 'til we drop,
For poetry's joyous and never will stop!

Sprig of the Spirit

In a tiny sprig of sage, humor dances bright,
It tickles the soul, a comical sight.
With a wink and a wiggle, it wobbles away,
Whispering secrets that brighten our day.

Each word like a petal, so light and so free,
Spreading the giggles like bees on a spree.
With roots in our hearts, and branches that sway,
Come gather 'round friends, let's laugh and play.

In the sun of the laughter, our spirits will soar,
Like dandelion wishes wafting ashore.
This sprig of delight, let it grow without bound,
For joy in a garden is all to be found.

So pluck this small giggle, and plant it in cheer,
Let it flourish and flourish, bring friends near.
In the garden of spirits, where silliness thrives,
We'll harvest the laughter and share our lives.

Lanterns of Language

In the twilight of thought, our lanterns ignite,
Words flicker and bounce, oh what a delight!
Each sentence a spark, illuminating the dark,
Casting shadows of giggles, a curious arc.

Jokes hang like lanterns, aglow with a grin,
They swing in the breeze, inviting us in.
So come, take a seat, let the stories unfold,
With laughter like fireflies, bright and bold.

Under the glow, our imaginations soar,
As language takes flight, who could ask for more?
So grab a hot cocoa, snuggle in tight,
For the lanterns of words will keep us alight.

In this garden of chatter, let the giggles burst,
With each flickering phrase, quenching our thirst.
A festival of language, it's quite the event,
Where laughter is king, and joy is content.

The Poetry of Pollinators

Bees buzz loudly, a dance in the air,
Fluttering flowers with a rhythm so rare.
They wear tiny suits, so dapper and neat,
Nature's own helpers, making life sweet.

In gardens they flit, with a flick of their wings,
Chasing the sunshine, oh what joy it brings!
With pollen they paint, in colors so bright,
Crafting a masterpiece, a floral delight.

But watch out, friend, don't get too close,
For when they get angry, they'll turn to their dose.
It's not just honey, it's a sticky affair,
A humor-filled drama, a show beyond compare.

So here's to the buzz, the fun in their flight,
Every little moment, a pure delight.
In gardens and fields, let laughter arise,
For poetry blooms under sunny blue skies.

Narrative in Nectar

The flowers whisper, in colors so bold,
Tales of the nectar, their stories unfold.
A drop of sweetness, they share with a sigh,
So tempting and tasty, it catches the eye.

A butterfly lands with a graceful ballet,
Sipping on sweetness, it's a fine buffet.
Each blossom a chapter, a tale to explore,
Dancing through gardens, each day brings more.

Ants march in line, a parade in the grass,
Carrying crumbs, oh they're quick and they're brash.
With laughter and crumbs, they party all night,
Storytellers of earth, in their own quirky flight.

So raise up a glass, to the buzz and the bloom,
To narratives sweet, that sparkle and zoom.
In every sip taken, a journey awaits,
Funny little tales of nectar-filled fates.

Growth of Grit

In cracks of the pavement, the wildflowers sprout,
With grit and with laughter, they dance all about.
A dandelion proud, with a puff and a grin,
Says, "Watch me take flight, I'm ready to win!"

The weeds join the fun, with their unkempt style,
Claiming the garden, with a cheeky smile.
Each leaf a reminder, a tale to be told,
Of strength in the struggle, and boldness in gold.

The squirrels and birds, they sit back and cheer,
As the flowers grow strong through the struggles they bear.
With laughter and roots, they dig in with pride,
Pushing through hardships, oh what a ride!

In every small shoot, there's humor and grit,
Life's patchwork quilt, with each little bit.
So here's to the blooms, against odds they insist,
Growing with laughter, in nature's twist.

Harmonies in Hedges

The hedges whisper, a tune to behold,
Where critters convene, both brave and bold.
Each rustle a note, each thump quite a sight,
As critters compose their symphony at night.

The hedgehogs glisten, with twinkling delight,
Their waltz in the twilight, a whimsical sight.
While foxes frolic, in mischievous play,
Creating a melody that brightens the day.

A chorus of frogs, with their croaks and their croons,
Becomes a unique ode to the light of the moon.
The crickets insist on their rhythmic refrain,
Turning the hedges into a musical lane.

So listen closely, to the quirk of the greens,
Where laughter persists, and joy intervenes.
In hedges and laughter, let friendships align,
For nature's a stage, where all souls intertwine.

Tending to Tinctures

In a pot of herbs, I found a rhyme,
A sprinkle of parsley, a pinch of lime.
With basil's giggle and thyme's soft sigh,
I make my potions as the daisies cry.

The mints are minty; they twist and twirl,
They whisper secrets in a leafy swirl.
Sage gives advice with a sage-like nod,
While cilantro dreams of a summer pod.

In each little sprout, a project too grand,
A chorus of flavors at my command.
I brew my concoctions with laughter and cheer,
As the garden hums in good natured sneer.

Now ready to sip on my herbal delight,
With each tiny drop, the world feels bright.
The funniest part? Not one drop's the same,
In this botanical dance, all pots play the game.

Whispers in the Terracotta

Terracotta pots with smiles so wide,
Hear the whispers of growth, they cannot hide.
A cactus cackles with prickly charm,
And ferns giggle softly, no need for alarm.

The daisies in clay pots, all in a row,
Play tag with the breezes, it's quite the show.
While the soil tells tales of what's yet to be,
Oh, the stories that bloom, if you'll just see!

Sunshine spills laughter on each little leaf,
Causing the bugs to dance in disbelief.
With bees in a buzz and butterflies bold,
My garden's a circus, a sight to behold!

So I sit with my mugs, tea warm in my hand,
Listening to whispers from this marvelous land.
In the joy of the pots, I find my own tune,
As the sunset drapes laughter over my commune.

Verses in Bloom

In the garden of giggles where daisies play,
Verses sprout swiftly, in a bright array.
The roses join in, they tenderly tease,
While tulips perform with the greatest of ease.

Nasturtiums chuckle as they bloom with flair,
And sunflowers wink, not a sorrow to share.
Every little bud has a story to tell,
In this patch of delight, all is quite swell.

The weeds are the jesters, they dance with glee,
Here in my garden, wild spirits roam free.
Every petal flips pages of poems untold,
With laughter, in colors, my heart can behold.

So let's gather round for a botanical jest,
With verses in bloom, life's an endless quest.
In this playful patch, let our spirits take flight,
As we craft witty lines from morning to night.

The Garden of Stanzas

In the garden of stanzas, oh what a sight,
Each plot's a new poem, each day is bright.
With laughter like daisies, and words that can soar,
Bulbs of wild humor are sprouting galore.

Hydrangeas giggle, and zinnias wink,
Bringing life to my lines with a chuckle and blink.
Every petal a page, every leaf a line,
In this sunny retreat, my musings entwine.

With carrots that rhyme and peas that make puns,
Even weeds in the corners can fetch lots of fun.
Rooted in laughter, their joy takes parade,
As I tend to their tales with a flip of a spade.

So join in the planting, let each stanza grow,
In the garden of wonders where laughter will flow.
With each little sprig, let imagination roam,
In this patch of creation, we'll always feel home.

Gardens of Verses

In my backyard, words grow tall,
With rhymes like weeds that never fall.
Each line a sprout, each word a seed,
Watered with laughter, they grow indeed.

Gnomes are my critics, they won't let me lie,
They chuckle and nod, with a glint in their eye.
Each pun's a petal, each joke's a root,
Digging for laughter, in my verbal loot.

I trim the syllables, prune them with care,
Plant metaphors round, give them fresh air.
As sunbeams scribble on pages of green,
My garden of verse is a whimsical scene.

So come take a stroll, through this jolly plot,
Where humor blooms brightly, and worries are naught.
With laughter like daisies, sprouting up high,
In this whimsical haven where words never die.

Whispers in Clay

Molding lines in the sun, so soft and bright,
A sculptor of phrases, oh what a sight!
With laughter I knead, and with joy I declare,
Each stanza I shape, is beyond compare.

The clay giggles back, with each little turn,
Crafting a punchline, oh how it does churn!
Fingers covered in ink, a playful mess,
Creating some verses, I must confess.

From clay pots sprout rhymes, they wiggle and spin,
A tangle of humor held deep within.
With each little twist, I'm cracking a smile,
A merry little dance, that goes on for a while.

In my studio's chaos, where laughter still plays,
I sculpt out my thoughts in delightful displays.
With whispers of clay, my verses do bloom,
In this funny little land, there's always more room.

Ink and Earth

There's ink on my hands, and dirt on my shoes,
A poet gardener, conspiring with blues.
Each word is a root, each rhyme a bright bud,
Sprinkled with giggles, and a dash of good mudd.

I plant all my verses in rows neat and fine,
With a shovel of humor, and rhythm divine.
The earth chuckles gently, as I dig for a punch,
Unearthing some laughter in a funny, loud crunch.

The quill dances lightly, all earthy and bold,
Sowing seeds of delight, each story retold.
With a breeze full of giggles, the pages take flight,
In this garden of nonsense, everything's bright.

The sun peeks through clouds, it's a laughter-filled sky,
While worms wiggle to rhythms, oh my, oh my!
With ink and with earth, my muse does reside,
In this quirky little garden, where joy's amplified.

The Blooming Stanza

In a pot of giggles, my stanzas reside,
Laid roots of nonsense, oh what a ride!
With blossoms of laughter, sprouting with glee,
Each line gets a chuckle, a sight to see.

The garden is buzzing with puns on the breeze,
While petals of humor float down with such ease.
I water the jokes till they bloom full and round,
A colorful chorus, where fun can be found.

With sunshine as ink, and rain clouds as rhyme,
Each stanza is crafted, in whimsical time.
The bees hum in rhythm, adding sweet flair,
In this blooming spectacle, I forget all my care.

So wander through verses, with a smile on your face,
In this garden of laughter, there's plenty of space.
For every pun whispered, and each clever jest,
The blooming stanza's a delightful fest!

Poetry in Petri Dishes

My rhymes grow slow, like mold on bread,
In science class, they dance instead.
With clever quips, and words like seeds,
They sprout up wild, satisfying needs.

In beakers bright and jars so neat,
Jokes bubble up, quite hard to beat.
Each strophe swells, a frothy mess,
I laugh so hard, I must confess.

The Potting Shed Serenade

In the shed, where plants do play,
The seedlings whisper jokes all day.
A cactus cracks a prickly pun,
While daisies laugh, 'Oh, what fun!'

The gardener hums a silly tune,
While marigolds sway, all in June.
They chat about the rain and sun,
In a patchwork world of garden fun.

Versified Vines

Vines climb high, and poets giggle,
Their verses sway, and gently wiggle.
With every twist, a punchline grows,
In tangled rhyme, humor flows.

Leaves adorned with puns so bright,
They tickle thoughts from morning light.
Twisting tales, they all create,
In winding paths, they celebrate.

Rhythms in Red Clay

In red clay pots, the rhythms play,
A chorus of plants in funny array.
With roots that dance beneath the ground,
They share their laughs without a sound.

The garden's glee, a funny sight,
As petals bloom, all colors bright.
In earthen homes, where humor grows,
Each heartbeat brings forth funny prose.

Blossoms of Breath

In a pot sat a cactus, quite shy,
Wishing for friends to flutter by.
Along came a fern, all frilly and bright,
"Why are you prickly? You're not in a fight!"

A daffodil added, with a giggle and sway,
"Join us for tea, it'll make your day!"
But alas, the poor cactus just stood in despair,
"I can't sip tea, I'm stuck in this chair!"

The soil began laughing, it shook with delight,
Watching the cactus in its plight.
With a wink and a grin, the blooms gave a cheer,
"Don't worry, dear cactus, you're safe here!"

And so in the pot, with smiles and some cheer,
The unlikely friends learned to persevere.
With blossoms of laughter, they flourished and grew,
In a garden of whimsy where dreams all come true.

The Terrace of Thought

On a terrace so sunny, thoughts took to flight,
Where daisies debated with all their might.
A dandelion shouted, "I'm fluffy and grand!"
While a shy little sprout felt too small to stand.

They giggled and squiggled, oh what a scene,
As roses rolled over, just feeling so keen.
"Let's throw a party, with cake made of dew!"
Chortled the lilac, "We're all invited too!"

The daisies danced wildly, the violets swayed,
The terrace transformed, a colorful parade.
And laughter rang loud, from weeds to the bloom,
As the sunflowers grinned from their leafy costume.

From thoughts light as air, the happiness grew,
In a patchwork of colors, every shade and hue.
The terrace of thoughts, oh, what joy it brings,
Where every flower bursts forth, and all nature sings.

Fragments in Flora

In a quirky garden, where shadows conspire,
Lived herbs with dreams that would always backfire.
A basil once whispered, "I want to be sage!"
But the rosemary scoffed, "You're far too too vague!"

Petunias in clusters told tales of the sky,
While one cheeky seedling said, "Why even try?"
"Just grow where you can, and reach for the sun!"
"But what if I flop, and it's not any fun?"

The gravel just chuckled beneath all the greens,
As petals exchanged their old gossiping scenes.
From fragments of flora, new stories take flight,
And laughter erupts in the warm morning light.

So if you find yourself lost in this place,
Just sit with the blooms, let them fill up your space.
For in this wild garden, all worries untie,
In fragments of flora, we learn how to fly.

Vines of Vibration

Up high in the trellis, where vines twist and sway,
The grapes started grooving, in a jolly ballet.
"Let's dance like the wind!" one grapelet proposed,
But the big grape just sighed, "I'm too round and dozed!"

The ivy chimed in, saying, "Join the fun, please!
We'll swirl and we'll twirl, like leaves in the breeze!"
So they jived all evening, while crickets provided,
A serenade sweet, that left no one quieted.

Even broccoli flopped in, quite late to the show,
"I'm here to be groovy, just don't step on my toe!"
The laughter erupted, the night full of glee,
As vegetables waltzed in pure jubilee.

And as morning approached, the revelers stretched,
A tapestry woven, from fun they had fetched.
With vines of vibration, each heart felt alive,
In this garden of joy, where laughter can thrive.

Fables from Fertile Ground

In the garden where gnomes dance,
A flower held a silly trance.
It sang with bees, quite out of tune,
As rabbits laughed beneath the moon.

A lettuce leaf wore a crown,
In broccoli, a king sat down.
They schemed to rule the veggie aisle,
While peas rolled on, laughing in style.

The carrots held a court so grand,
With radish knights at their command.
Each tale of veggies spun so bright,
Kept friends and critters up all night.

In this patch of joy, it's clear,
Nature's tales bring endless cheer.
With roots and rhymes intertwined,
Fables bloom in hearts and mind.

Lyrical Lushness

A sunflower sways with flair,
As daisies gossip in the air.
They trade their jokes, both sweet and bright,
While tulips giggle, feeling light.

The ivy's climb a crafty scheme,
It winks at moss, "We're quite the team!"
In shadows, ferns dance on their toes,
While daisies shake in their fine clothes.

A plantain leaf tells jokes on leaves,
While rooting for a garden of thieves.
"Come join the fun!" the marigold calls,
As laughter echoes through the walls.

So let us toast to blooms and greens,
In whimsical worlds where joy convenes.
With petals bright and spirits high,
In lyrical lushness, let's all fly!

Syllables in the Sunlight

The sun spills gold on lilacs near,
While dandelions grin with cheer.
Each petal turns a giggling page,
In nature's book, we find our stage.

Bumblebees buzz with comic flair,
Telling tales of their sweet affair.
With pollen hats and fuzzy suits,
They dance along in whimsical boots.

Tomatoes blush like shy debutantes,
While carrots share their funny haunts.
Every sprout waits for the sun,
In rhymes of laughter, life's pure fun.

So gather 'round, oh friends of mine,
In leafy laughter, let's entwine.
With sunlight's touch, and glee in bloom,
We sway together, banish gloom.

Evergreen Echoes

Amidst the pines where whispers play,
A squirrel jokes to start the day.
With acorns stacked in towers high,
He plans a feast beneath the sky.

The cedar shakes with giggles low,
While ferns share secrets, oh so slow.
As moss creates a comfy bed,
Dreams of mischief dance in their head.

A chat between the roots and dirt,
"Let's spread the word and be absurd!"
The wind composes tunes of cheer,
As laughter rings for all to hear.

In this evergreen, our hearts unite,
With echoes of joy, soft and light.
So sway along, let spirits mend,
In nature's jokes, let laughter blend.

www.ingramcontent.com/pod-product-compliance
Lightning Source LLC
Chambersburg PA
CBHW072126070526
44585CB00016B/1561